Rookie
Read-About® Math

Is It Still a Number?

WITHDRAWN

By Pam Rosenberg

Subject Consultant
Chalice Bennett
Elementary Specialist
Martin Luther King Jr. Laboratory School
Evanston, Illinois

Reading Consultant
Cecilia Minden-Cupp, PhD
Former Director, Language and Literacy Program
Harvard Graduate School of Education

Children's Press®
A Division of Scholastic Inc.
New York Toronto London Auckland Sydney
Mexico City New Delhi Hong Kong
Danbury, Connecticut

Designer: Herman Adler Design
Photo Researcher: Caroline Anderson
The photo on the cover shows a brother and sister playing with
magnetic numbers.

Library of Congress Cataloging-in-Publication Data

Rosenberg, Pam.
  Is it still a number? / by Pam Rosenberg.
    p. cm. — (Rookie read-about math)
  Includes index.
  ISBN10: 0-516-25443-X (lib. bdg.)   0-516-25594-0 (pbk.)
  ISBN13: 978-0-516-25443-2 (lib. bdg.)   978-0-516-25594-1 (pbk.)
  1. Number concept—Juvenile literature. 2. Numeracy—Juvenile literature.
3. Arithmetic—Juvenile literature. I. Title. II. Series.
  QA141.15.R67 2006
  513–dc22   2005035813

CHILDREN'S PRESS, and ROOKIE READ-ABOUT®,
and associated logos are trademarks and/or registered trademarks
of Scholastic Library Publishing. SCHOLASTIC and associated logos
are trademarks and/or registered trademarks of Scholastic Inc.

1 2 3 4 5 6 7 8 9 10 R 16 15 14 13 12 11 10 09 08 07   08

I like to help my little brother learn about numbers.

He knows all about
numbers that look
like this: 14.

fourteen

14

One morning, we were reading a book. I read the word *fourteen*. He asked, "Is that a number?" I said, "Yes! Fourteen is the same as 14."

My brother asked me if there were other ways to show the number fourteen. "Sure," I said. "I'll show you some of them."

9

"Your birthday is in two weeks," I said to my brother. "That's 7 + 7 days. Seven plus seven is another name for fourteen."

"Get some blocks," I said to my brother. "Stack up ten of them. Now stack up four more. Put the two piles next to each other. Can you count how many blocks are in the stacks?"

"Now get your piggy bank. Open it up and find one dime and four pennies. That's fourteen cents. You can write it like this: 14¢."

It was time for lunch. My brother asked, "Is twelve o'clock a number?"

I told him the number 12 told us what hour it was on the clock. The zeros told us how many minutes past the hour it was. It was exactly twelve o'clock.

My brother ran out of the room. He came back with Dad's watch.

"Why doesn't Dad's watch say twelve o'clock?" he asked. "It has funny writing on it."

I laughed. "It sure does,"
I said. "Those are numbers,
too. They are called
Roman numerals. *Numeral*
is another way of saying
'numbers.' Twelve looks
like this." I wrote *XII*.

"Is that really a number?"
he asked. "It sure is!"
I said.

"The *X* is a symbol for 10, and each *I* stands for 1. So *XII* is 10 + 1 + 1 = 12."

Mom made soup and a sandwich for lunch. My brother and I each ate half a sandwich.

My brother asked if one-half was a number. I said it was. I wrote the number $\frac{1}{2}$. I told him it was called a *fraction*.

A fraction means we broke a whole number down to smaller parts, just as we cut the whole sandwich into two smaller parts. He said fractions were yummy!

We have a bird feeder in our backyard. After lunch, my brother wanted to count how many birds he saw. I helped him by making a tally box.

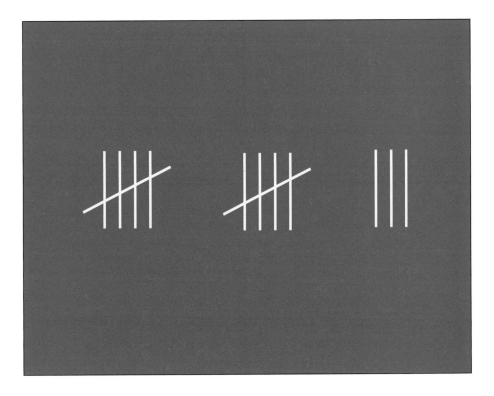

I showed my brother how many birds we saw. He looked confused. "That's not a number!" he said.

I explained how to count up the tally marks. "It is a number," he said with a smile. "It's the number 13. We saw thirteen birds!"

Numbers don't always look the same, but they are still numbers.

How many numbers have you seen today?

29

Words You Know

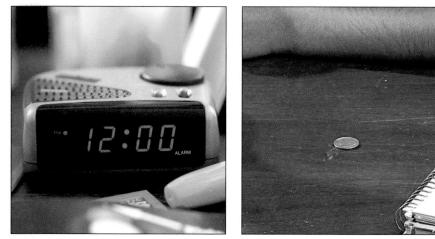

clock

dime

fraction

number

pennies

tally marks

Roman numerals

Index

About the Author

Pam Rosenberg is a writer and editor. She lives near Chicago, Illinois, with her husband and two children who like learning about numbers.

Photo Credits